YOUR KNOWLEDGE H

Bibliographic information published by the German National Library:

The German National Library lists this publication in the National Bibliography; detailed bibliographic data are available on the Internet at http://dnb.dnb.de .

Imprint:

Copyright © 2015 GRIN Verlag, Open Publishing GmbH
Print and binding: Books on Demand GmbH, Norderstedt Germany
ISBN: 9783668243729

This book at GRIN:

http://www.grin.com/en/e-book/334705/social-mobility-in-the-elite-to-what-extent-does-the-probability-of-attaining

Sebastian Steidle

Social mobility in the elite. To what extent does the probability of attaining elite positions depend on elite origins?

GRIN Publishing

GRIN - Your knowledge has value

Since its foundation in 1998, GRIN has specialized in publishing academic texts by students, college teachers and other academics as e-book and printed book. The website www.grin.com is an ideal platform for presenting term papers, final papers, scientific essays, dissertations and specialist books.

Visit us on the internet:

http://www.grin.com/

http://www.facebook.com/grincom

http://www.twitter.com/grin_com

rhard Karls Universität Tübingen
itut für Soziologie

08.04.2015

Recruitment, Reproduction and Circulation of the Elite

Seminar: Social Mobility

eidle, Sebastian

Contents

1. Introduction

In the fall of 2016, a new president of the United States of America will be elected.. At this time, according to bookmakers[1], the most likely scenario is a race between the Governor of Florida, Jeb Bush and Hillary Rodham Clinton, the current U.S. Secretary of State.

The citizens of the of the United States would have to choose between a son and brother of a former president and the wife of a former president. Whoever would make the race, the allocation of the arguably most powerful position in the world, would be an extreme case of intra-familiar inheritance. Even though this scenario is not more than a speculation yet, its relatively high likelihood of occurrence, can be seen as a contradiction to the crucial American self-perception as an open and meritocratic nation.[2] Of course a single social position or event does not tell us much about the condition of a society, but it raises the question, to what extend power is inherited in western societies.

Since C. Wright Mills' "The Power Elite" (1956/2000), questions about the composition and cohesion of the top level of the stratification hierarchy, and also about the mechanisms behind recruitment to this level, have been central. This paper will examine different questions regarding elite recruitment. Firstly, what are the patterns of elite recruitment; does this level consist of separate elites or a common class? Do the different elite groupings vary with respect to degree of openness, i.e. what is the degree of elite mobility? In other words, to what extent does the probability of attaining elite positions depend on social origins, and more specifically, on elite origins? How important are economical, cultural and social resources for elite recruitment? Is there a development towards more openness or are there trends pointing in the opposite direction?

This issue is important out of several reasons. Since it was observed, that even communist societies develop an extensive elite in form of party officials, it is widely believed, that the existence of some sort of ruling class is unavoidable in a modern mass society.[3] Modern day policy doesn't lay the focus on the equality of outcome, but on the equality of opportunity instead. In a society with egalitarian values, the existence of an elite must be legitimized over merit and the effectiveness the society aspects from a chosen class. The perception, that elite

---

[1] http://www.oddschecker.com/politics/us-politics/us-presidential-election-2016/betting-markets (14.3.2015)
[2] In the public perception, Barack Obama is sometimes seen as an example to show the opposite or even as a personification of the the American Dream. While his election may indicate, that everyone can become president in terms of racial background, his election is not a strong argument for the irrelevance of social background. His father holds a Masters Degree in economics from Harvard University and his mother had a Doctor of Philosophy in anthropology. Most of his childhood he lived with his grandfather -a successful salesman- and his grandmother -the former vice president of the Bank of Hawaii. From fifth grade on, he attended to a private school. (Maraniss: 2012)
[3] An observation first noticed by the sociologist Robert Michels, which he introduced as „the iron law of oligarchy" (1915)

3

positions are allocated in an open and fair contest is of normative meaning in a democracy (cf. Turner 1994: 260f.). The rate of social mobility in elite circles could even be seen as the one sole thing, that differentiates a democracy from an oligarchy. The normative, as the pragmatic legitimization can suffer from low mobility rates. It's argued that low mobility rates are indicating, that class positions are not allocated by merit but by heritage instead. Therefore a lot of talent under individuals with the wrong heritage is wasted and the efficiency of elite decisions are suffering.

Another reason why it is essential to look closer on the elite, is, that social background not only has a strong influence on the own social position, but also on the system of values and the worldview a person has, as well as on the social attachment he or she feels. Therefore low rates of mobility within the elite can lead to an ideological gap and missing social cohesion between the elite and masses. For example a executive manager or politician who grew up in a working class family, will probably not only still feel some sort of affiliation with his class of origin but has also a better understanding of the way blue-collar worker are seeing the world. Furthermore he could emphasis his perception in his new peer group.[4] A closed elite tends to concentrate solidarity within the own box, while jeopardizing the the social bonds with the masses (cf. Sorokin 1994: 248ff.). According to Vilfredo Pareto (1916/1961), a society, where the elite is self-reproducing, use to be rigid and not able to react to social change in a adequate manner. This would lead to a revolution where the elite is overthrown in a violent way. In a open society, on the other hand, where the elite is recruited out of the most capable in all classes, a equilibrium would be retained. How diverse the elite really is and how much homogenity is necessary for the elite to be functioning, are two widely debated questions (cf. Hoffmann-Lange 2003: 111ff.). To some extend, ideological cleavages and a lack of solidarity do exist between all social groups and tend to get stronger with the seclusiveness of the groups (Vgl. Sorokin 1994: 248ff.), but in this case, they are particularly critical, because of the elites ability to impose their own will on society as a whole. They are able to shape the national culture and institutions in a way that they fit their own values and interests (cf. Davidson/Pyle 751). At least in pluralistic understanding of democracy, power should be divided between different competing groups and that generally binding decision should balance the conflicting interests of these opposing groups (Hoffmann-Lange 2003: 111ff.). Representative democracies are based on the principal, that national decision should

---

[4]According to Lipset (1994: 256f.) this depends on how big the cultural differences between classes in a society are. While in the USA, a country with a strong ideology of egalitarianism and small cultural differences between the classes, achievers tend to become more conservative, in middle and northern European countries, where the cultural differences between the classes are bigger, upward mobile persons tend to support left-wing parties.

reflect a cross section of society or the society as a whole.[5] Therefore, the immobility of the elite could effect the legitimation of the elite.[6]

2. Research

Unlike other class conceptions in social stratification research, the category "elite" usually isn't defined over income, occupation or prestige, but over the concept of power (which typically rests upon wealth, occupation or prestige). Studies in Elite Research vary in the breadth of their conceptualisation of the elite. In the close and classic definition of Mills (1956/2000: 18), the elite includes "those political, economic, and military circles, which as an intricate set of overlapping small but dominant groups share decisions having at least national consequences." Besides this "triangle of Power" (ibid.: 8) consisting out of the commanders in the mayor political, economic and military institutions, other studies have a broader understanding of the elite and include the highest positions in the judiciary, diplomatic service, churches and trade unions as well as the most influential persons in the fields of mass media, culture and science. This elitist groups show quite different selection mechanisms. One pattern is, that the more people decide over the allocation of the elite position (for instance in a democratic election) or the more formalized the allocation of the position is (for instance in a highly bureaucratic institution), the more unimportant the social background gets. Another pattern is, that the closer the elite is defined or the higher the elite position is, the more more homogeneous the group gets in their social origin and the better the elite can be understood as a network of informal connections and shared interests.

Elite research results are hardly quantitatively comparable. First, because a lot researches focussing on one specific elitist group and second, because even by trying to look at the elite as a whole, the elite can, depending on the definition, include different elitist groups and can in a society numerically range from a few hundred persons into the millions (Dogan 2003: 28/32/62).

In Germany, there has been two big elite surveys, most research on the field is based upon: The Mannheim Elite Study 1981 (Kaase et.al. 1981) and the Potsdam Elite Study 1995 (Schnapp et.al. 1997). Unfortunately, due to the different design of the surveys, a systematized comparison over time is difficult and there has been no major survey since and the German

---

[5] For the same reason, countries like Germany for example have introduced gender quotas for supervisory boards and all major German political parties have gender quotas for some office positions.

[6] In recent years, several political movements arose, who operate with an harsh anti-elite rhetoric. Right-wing populist movements like the American Tea Party or the French Front National as well as left-wing populist movements like Occupy Wall Street or the Greek Syriza. All of them claim, that the elites can't or won't understand the sorrows and problems of the common man. (cf.: Priester 2012: 222)

elite research seem to have come to a stagnation in past years. Outside of Germany, the composition and recruitment of the elite seems of high concern for British and French sociologists, and is usually seen in the context of their system of elite education (e.g. Griffiths et. al. 2014, Brezis/Hellier 2013, Dogan 2003, Tholen 2013), while I could find relatively less results for the United States (e.g. Carroll 2010). A lot of elite research is qualitative oriented and examines the networks and habits within the elite and elite universities.

2.1 The Different Sectors of the Elite

A lot of elite researches like Useem (1984), Dogan (2003) and Krysmanski (2007) conceptualise the elite in a ring model. In the innermost ring is the money elite or the super rich. A group that can start, depending on the definition, by an wealth of 30 million dollars (estimated 167,000 globally in 2014; West 2014: 116) or not until 1 billion dollars (estimated 1,682 globally in 2014; ibid.). The second ring of the elite consists out of the highest ranking positions in politics, the military, the judiciary and the corporate world. Hartmann (2001) found for Germany, that in this group, the social descent plays the biggest role for the business elite, followed by the elites in military and the judicial system. For members of the government, the social heritage plays a relatively unimportant role. Hartmann showed, that even when education plays an increasing role in the elite recruitment, that in all these sectors, a direct effect of class background could be found. He also found, that also in the outer ring of the elite, members with an upper class heritage are significantly overrepresented – except for union leaders and the political elite of left-leaning parties. But the effect of class background pretty much fades, when for higher officials and the media elite, when its only looked at members with a doctorate, which more than half of the elite possess. In the field of science, the middle-class children who made a doctorate, are overrepresented. Grifith et. al. (2008, 2014) suggests similar sectorial patterns for Great Britain.

For Hartmann, this can be explained with the career choices of the upper-class, who prefers more lucrative positions. Because economic elite makes up about two thirds of the elite (Hartmann 2007) and the class heritage plays at the same time a creator role in this sectors, it's worthwhile to take a closer look on the economic elites.

2.2 The Money Elite

Among all elitist groups, the very rich have the lowest level of education and the lowest rates of mobility at the same time. This is simply because their wealth is to a large extend "inherited", in the traditional meaning of the word, and kept together by an high rate of endogamy (Dogan 2003: 32; Krysmanski 2007: 1008). According to West (2014: 148f.) 65 percent of the 492 Billionaires in the U.S. today have their origins in the upper class. Out of these 65 percent a third of where born in a billionaire family, another third inherited at least a part of their wealth, while the remaining third originated in the upper-class without being inheritors. This corresponds to the results of Keister (2005), who found, by examining the *Forbes 400 Richest Americans of 2002*, that 63 percent of the people listed had inherited a noteworthy proportion of their wealth (in contrast to 68 percent in 1982).

This composition, with only about 35 percent of the super rich having a lower-class or middle-class background, shows some persistence over time. According to Mills (1956/2000: 105), in the year 1950, of the 275 Americans with a fortune of at least 30 million Dollars, 68 percent grew up in the upper class. 93 percent of this 68 percent where inheritors (ibid.: 107). Besides the 62 percent of very rich with relatives among the very rich of previous generations, farmers, white collar- and blue collar workers   combined, smaller entrepreneurs and professionals, each make up for about 10 percent of the father's occupational statuses (ibid.: 105). The relative constant share of upper class within the very rich and the decreased share inheritors between 1950 and 2014 stands in contrast to the increasing influence of social background Mills discovered for the years between 1900, where only 39 percent of the very rich originated from the upper class and 1950. It seems that, while the disparities of wealth distribution between the very rich and the rest of society have gotten bigger (Atkinson et al. 2011) in the last 65 years, the mobility between these two groups has increased at the same time. Apparently, the tendency of wealth, claimed by Mills, not only to perpetuate itself but also "to monopolize new opportunities for getting great wealth" (1956/2000: 105) has weakened. This may have at least partly to do with the appearance of new technologies and the so called "dot-com billionaires". From the slightly weakening effect of inherited fortune, primarily the outer circle of the upper class benefited. It seems, that even under the so called self-made man, receiving some start-up capital from a family member and having the right connections plays a big role in creating vast wealth (cf. Keister: 2005)[7]

---

[7]The unknown programmer and Harvard dropout Bill Gates wouldn't be the the wealthiest man in the world today, if it wasn't for his mother Mary, who served on several major cooperation's boards. At a time where I.B.M was in search for a operating system for their Personal Computer, he probably would have never attracted the companie's attention, if Mary Gates hadn't mentioned her son's name to her fellow member on

2.3 The Business Elite

Hartmann (2007) found, that in France, Britain and Germany, more than 50 percent of the top executives, managers and business professionals have their social origin in the grand bourgeoisie. This class, consisting out of academical freelancers, high officials and officers, larger entrepreneurs and executive managers, made up for only about 3.5 percent of society in the father's generation.

Griffiths et. al. (2010) examined the 100 largest French and British companies and their directors between 1998 and 2003. They found, using the Halsey (1995) classification for social origins (upper, upper-middle, lower-middle and lower), that in both countries a majority of the top 100 directors were raised in upper or upper-middle class households: 77% of French cases and 64 % of the British. Likewise, 95% of the French attended an elite school (especially the top Parisian lycées), while 88% of the British attended an independent or grammar school. Afterwards, nearly all of the top 100 directors in French, and most of the top 100 directors in Britain attended to a elite university. Further they found, that 84 of the top 100 British directors began their carrer in the corporate sector, while 49 of their French counter-parts began their careers in government service, compared to 41 in the corporate sector.

This corresponds to the findings of Hartmann (2007), that in France, almost all top positions in almost all important sectors are taken up by graduates of the Grand Ecole. For the United Kingdom he found a similar but slightly less strong pattern. Although, these schools produce more graduates and are slightly less socially homogeneous.

Most literature suggests, that social background in access to elite positions has slightly lessens its importance over the past fiew decades, and that education and qualification has gained importance (Schnapp 1997, Ruostetsaari 2006, Griffiths et al. 2008, Carroll 2010). Most research corresponds in the finding, that social closure being very gradually attenuated over time amongst both private and public Elites (Keating and Cairney 2006; Griffiths et al. 2008), albeit maintaining an over-representation of those from privileged schools (Maclean et al. 2010; Hill 2013).

In the modernization theory, it is argued, that the increase in bureaucratization and technical specialization in a more and more increasingly complex economy, merit rather than family prestige facilities professional advancement and that education becoming a signifier of ability or productivity.

---

the executive committee of United Way, John Opel, then CEO of I.B.M.
(http://www.nytimes.com/1994/06/11/obituaries/mary-gates-64-helped-her-son-start-microsoft.html)

In Bourdieu's work (i.e. 1984), educational credentials are seen as being of rising importance in the reproduction of the upper class and a increasing source of distinction. But even when the social background operates transmitted through education, it's not necessarily an evidence for the meritocratic foundation of the elite. First, several studies suggest (i.e. Meulemann: 1991), that that the the effect of social background on educational achievement success is not completely transmitted through merit, but does have partly an direct influence. Therefore, recruiters favour candidates who went to the same or a similar school than themselves (Tholen et. al. 2013). Second, education provides - next to beeing born in the same upper class - not just one of the major sources of unity and homogenity among the elite, but also a major source for social capital, especially through contacts made in elite universities and high quality internships (ibid.)

Brezis and Hellier (2013) showed, that the higher the difference in expenditure per student between the elite and standard universities, the lower the upward social mobility of the middle class is, and the more self-reproducing the elite group gets.

Hartmann (2007) argues, that for the same reason, the tripartited school system in Germany, is leading to a relative high level of immobility for the society overall, the low share of boarding schools, private schools, private universities and the complete abstinence of elite universities[8], causes a relative openness of the elite. But even with the opening of universities for large segments of the population and the abstinence of elite universities, the German upper class found new ways to distinct themselves from the middle class educationally: By choosing law, economics or engineering as their field of studies, attend in high quality internships and doing a doctorate.

Hartmann (ibid.) identifies three main types of elite formation across the western world: a) A French model, with homogeneous elite recruitment through elite educational institutions (in particular the Grandes Écoles) and strong sectorial circulation, meaning that over their careers, the same persons circulate between leading positions in multiple sectors. b) An Anglo-saxon model, with elite recruitment through boarding schools, elite universities (in particular Oxford and Cambridge for the UK and the Ivy League Colleges in the US) and military institutions (Sandhurst in the UK and West Point in the US). The Anglo-Saxon model features a relatively homogeneous elite, but with a limited degree of sectorial circulation. And c): A German model, with relatively heterogeneous elite recruitment and limited sectorial circulation.

---

[8] In 1981 and 1995 no single university was significantly overrepresented among the German elite (Schnapp 1997)

3. The Glass Ceiling

Even when its seems, that elite positions are mainly allocated through educational attainment, and that the access to high educational attainment has gradually opened up for the middle-class, most elite researchers agree, that even when education is controlled, gender, the racial, religious and class background has a direct influence on ones changes to hold an elite position. The phenomena, that women, ethnic minorities and people with an non-upper class heritage are significantly underrepresented in elite positions, is known as "Glass Ceiling".

Because power is a key feature of the elite, more than any other class, the established elite self-co-opt its new recruits. The elite cannot only be seen as a class, but also as tight and interdependent network, even across sectorial and national borders (cf. Münkler et. Al: 2006). According to Hartmann (2001: 184ff.), the elite recognizes itself as community of fate, who succeeds or fails together. Therefore, trust and homogeneity are seen as crucial for the elite's efficiency. Tohlen et. al. (2013) argue, that prefer candidates, who share the same ideology, individual characteristics, demographic traits and went to same or a similar school than themselves. Therefore, cultural differences help explain the perpetuation of inequality by invisibly limiting access to elite cultural norms. Besides the lack of the right cultural capital and habitus, social capital is a reason for the homogenity of the elite. Economic elite positions are usually not advertised in the newspaper, but rather given away through personal contacts. Professionals primarily depend on their set of personal contacts to get information about job-chances opportunities rather than more formal or impersonal routes. According to Tholen et. al. (2013), 65% of all managerial workers found their job through social contacts. In a lot of cases, elite universities are serving – besides class consciousness - as an creator of such contacts and networks. The American elite, has been traditionally dominated by male Anglo-Saxon Protestants, especially of Presbyterian, Anglican and Congregationalist denomination. 95 percent of the man who signed United States Declaration of Independence and 85 percent of the delegates in Constitutional Convention of 1787 had been members of the "Protestant Establishment (Davidson/Pyle 2011). According to Davidson and Pyle, between 1800 and 1899 Anglicans, Congregationalists and Presbyterians made up for 56% of all governmental, industrial and university leaders, while having a population share of about 7%. That means, they where overrepresented among the elite by a ratio of 8 to 1 (versus 10 to 1 in the colonial period). While occasional accompanied by other protestant groups like Unitarians and Quakers, non-protestant groups like Catholics, Jews and non-religious affiliates had little chances to climb into the elite. The dominance of the protestant establishment in the elite continued in the early 20. century but started to crumble since 1950. The G.I. Bill of Rights of

1946 broke down ethnic barriers to college opportunities. In the 1960es the most prestigious schools implemented selective admissions criteria, which made it increasingly difficult for academically mediocre upper-class males to gain admissions to finer schools and eliminated informal religious quotas who served the purpose to keep Jews and Catholics away (Pyle 1996: 6. Between 1930 and 1990 the different Christian denominations slowly approached correspondence between their representation in the elite and the whole population. On the basis of "Who is Who in America" the odds ratio of catholic being in the elite rose from 0.13 in 1931 to 0.94. Even with dropping rates, the protestant establishment where highly overrepresented in 1993 by occupying 35.14 percent of all elite positions while at the same time making up for only about 6 percent of the total population today. A complete turnaround in the changes of occupying an elite position could be examined in the Jewish population, who went from being underrepresented in the elite with an odds ratio of 0.73 in 1931 to being overrepresented by the factor of 2.4 in 1993 (Ibid.). It seems like the admission requirement for the U.S elite has changed from being member of the male Anglo-Saxon Protestant establishment to being white male member of a Judeo-Christian church. In the United States, Hindus, Buddhists, Moslems, African-Americans, as well as women, are all underrepresented in the Money Elite by at least the factor of 7 (Keister 2005) and under the top 1000 CEOs and in the U.S. Congress by at least the factor of 5 (Davidson/Pyle 2011).

Bibliography

Atkinson, Anthony B. / Piketty, Thomas / Saez Emmanuel (2011): *Top incomes in the long run of history*. In: *Journal of Economic Literature*, 49 (1), (pp 3-71)

Bourdieu, Pierre (1984): *Distinction*. London: Routledge.

Brezis, Elise S./Hellier, Joël (2013): *Social Mobility at the Top: Why are Elites self-reproducing?* proposed for publication to *The American Economic Journal: Macroeconomics*

Carroll, W. K. (2010): *The Making of the Transnational Capitalist Class*. New York, NY: Zed Books.

Davidson, James D./Ralph E. Pyle (2011). *Ranking Faiths: Religious Stratification in American Society*. New York

Dogan, Mattei (2003): *Diversity of Elite Configurations and Clusters of Power*. In: Dogan, M. (ed.). *Elite Configurations at the Apex of Power*. Leiden, Boston: Brill, (pp.1-15)

Griffiths, D./Miles, A/Savage, M. (2008): *The end of the English cultural elite?* In: *Sociological Review* 56, (pp. 187–209)

Griffiths, Dave/Lambert, Paul S./Bihagen, Erik (2014): *Measuring the Potential Power Elite in the UK and Sweden*. In: *Organization Studies*, 31(03), (pp. 327–348)

Hartmann, Michael (2001): *Klassenspezifischer Habitus oder exklusive Bildungstitel als Selektionskriterium? Die Besetzung von Spitzenpositionen in der Wirtschaft*. In: Krais, Beate (Hrsg.). *An der Spitze. Deutsche Eliten im sozialen Wandel*. Konstanz, (pp. 157-215)

Hartmann, Michael (2007): *Eliten und Macht in Europa. Ein internationaler Vergleich*. Campus Verlag, Frankfurt am Main

Hoffmann-Lange, Ursula (2003): *Das pluralistische Paradigma der Elitenforschung*. In: Hradil, Sefan/Imbusch, Peter (ed.). *Oberschichten — Eliten — Herrschende Klassen*. Frankfurt/M.-New York, (pp 111-118)

Kaase, Max/Wildenmann, Rudolf (1981): *Führungsschicht in der Bundesrepublik Deutschland* (Mannheimer Elite-Studie 1981). GESIS Datenarchiv, Köln.

Keister, Lisa A. (2005): *Getting Rich. America's New Rich and How They Got That Way*. Cambridge

Krymanski, Hans-Jürgen (2007): *Der stille Klassenkampf von oben. Strukturen und Akteure des Reichtums*. In: *UTOPIE kreativ*, H. 205 (November), (pp. 999-1011)

Lipset, Seymor Martin/Bendix, Reinhard/Zetterberberg, Hans L. (1994): *Social and Cultural Mobility*. In: Grusky, D.B.(ed.). *Social Stratification in Sociological Perspective. Class, Race and Gender*. Boulder, Oxford: Westview Press. (pp. 250-259)

Maraniss, David (2012): *Barack Obama. The Story*. Simon & Schuster, New York City

Robert Michels (2009): *Political Parties*. Transaction Publishers. London [1915]

Ruostetsaari, I. (2006): *Social upheaval and transformations of elite structures: The case of Finland*. In: *Political Studies* 54 (pp. 23–42)

Mills, C. W. (2000): *The Power Elite*. Oxford University Press, New York [1956]

Meulemann, Heiner (1995): *Gleichheit und Leistung nach der Bildungsexpansion*. In: Reuband, Karl-Heinz/Pappi, Franz U./Best, Heinrich (ed.). *Die deutsche Gesellschaft in vergleichender Perspektive*. Festschrift für Erwin K. Scheuch zum 65. Geburtstag. Opladen: Westdeutscher Verlag. (pp. 207–220)

Münkler, Herfried/Bohlender, Matthias/Strassenberger, Grit: *Einleitung*. In: Münkler, Herfried/ Bohlender, Matthias/Strassenberger, Grit (ed.): *Deutschlands Eliten im Wandel*. Campus. Frankfurt am Main, (pp. 11-21)

Pareto, Vilfredo: *The Circulations of Elites (1961)*. In: Parsons, Talcott. *Theories of Society; Foundations of Modern Sociological Theory*. 2 Vol., The Free Press of Glencoe, Inc., (pp. 551-557),[1916]

Priester, Karin (2012): *Rechter und linker Populismus. Annäherung an ein Chamäleon*. Campus, Frankfurt am Main

Sorokin, Pitirim A.: Social and Cultural Mobility (pp. 245-250). In: Grusky, D.B. (1994). *Social Stratification in Sociological Perspective. Class, Race and Gender*. Boulder, Oxford: Westview Press.

Schnapp, Kai-Uwe/Welzel, Christian/Rebenstorf, Hilke/Kaina, Viktoria/Sauer, Martina/Machatzke, Jörg/Bürklin, Wilhelm (1997): *Eliten in Deutschland*. München

Tholen, Gerbrand/Brown, Philip/Power, Sally/Allouch, Annabelle (2013): *The role of networks and connections in educational elites' labour market entrance*. In: Research in Social Stratification and Mobility. 34, (pp. 142-154)

Turner, Ralph H. (1994): *Sponsored and Contested Mobility and the School System*. In: Grusky, D.B.. *Social Stratification in Sociological Perspective. Class, Race and Gender*. Boulder, Oxford: Westview Press., (pp. 260-264)

Useem, Michael (1984): *The Inner Circle: Large Corporations and the Rise of Business Political Activity*. New York: Oxford University Press.

West, Darrell M. (2014): *Billionaires - Reflections on the Upper Crust*. The Brookings Institution. Washington D.C.

Internet resources

http://www.oddschecker.com/politics/us-politics/us-presidential-election-2016/betting-markets (last retrieved: 14.03.2015)

http://www.nytimes.com/1994/06/11/obituaries/mary-gates-64-helped-her-son-start-microsoft.html (last retrieved: 18.03.2015)